Alfred's Basic Piano Li

Merry Christmas!

Willard A. Palmer ◆ Morton Manus ◆ Amanda Vick Lethco

Level 4

This book may be used with Level 4, or 5th book of any method.

CONTENTS

FOREWORD

Piano students and teachers alike look forward to the Christmas season, when they may have the pleasure of enjoying some of their favorite carols. These much-loved pieces provide motivation and variety that combine to enhance piano study, particularly when these selections are graded so as to reinforce exactly the principles that are being taught at the time they are assigned. With ALFRED'S BASIC PIANO LIBRARY, the student progresses each year to more advanced, fuller sounding versions of the carols, and these pieces become appropriate and important supplementary material.

The pieces are arranged in progressive order, and each one has an optional DUET PART, playable at the same piano. Measures are numbered to make practicing the duets easier.

The authors congratulate you for moving on to this new level, and wish you a MERRY CHRISTMAS. They also hope you will enjoy these new and special arrangements, and that they will bring pleasure to everyone who hears you play them!

Deck the Hall with Boughs of Holly

Traditional

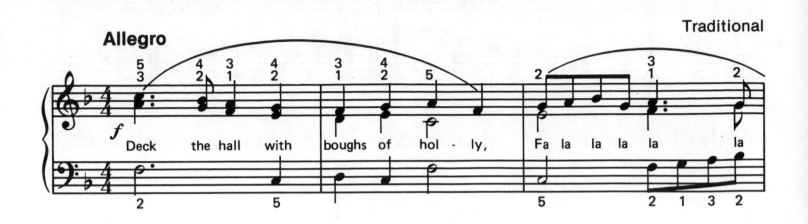

Deck the hall with boughs of hol - ly, Fa la la la la la

DUET PART: (Student plays 1 octave higher.)

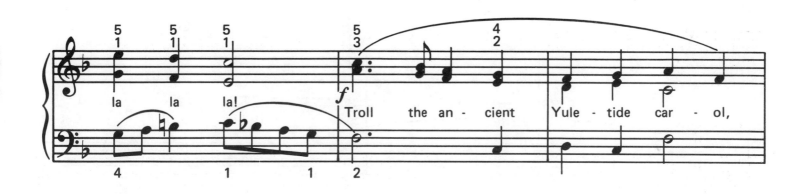

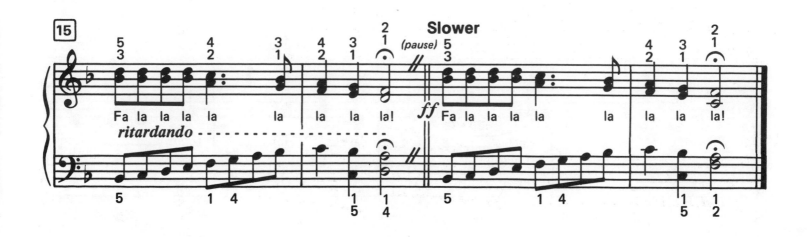

Joy to the World

G. F. Handel

Maestoso

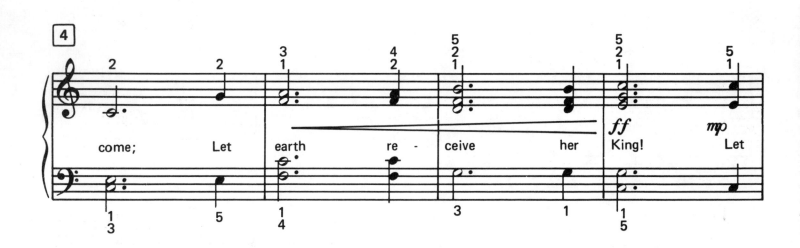

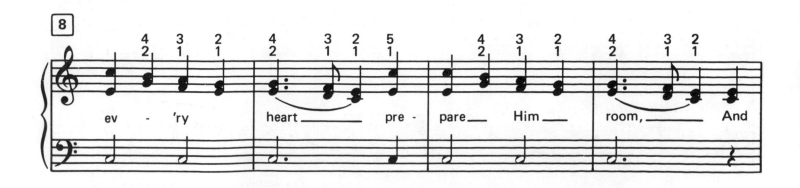

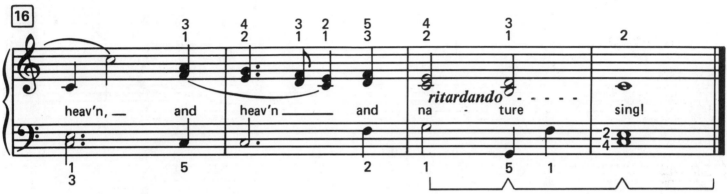

DUET PART:

Maestoso

Play this part 8va throughout.

ritardando - - - - - - - - - - - - - - -

Mary's Cradle Song

In this piece the left hand plays an *ostinato* (the same measure repeated over and over) imitating the rocking of the cradle. All three-note chords in the right hand are 1st inversion triads!

Traditional

*NOTE: The blurred sounds caused by holding the pedal through the chord changes gives an "impressionistic effect," and is intentional. The piece must be played very quietly. At no time should the volume be louder than *mp*.

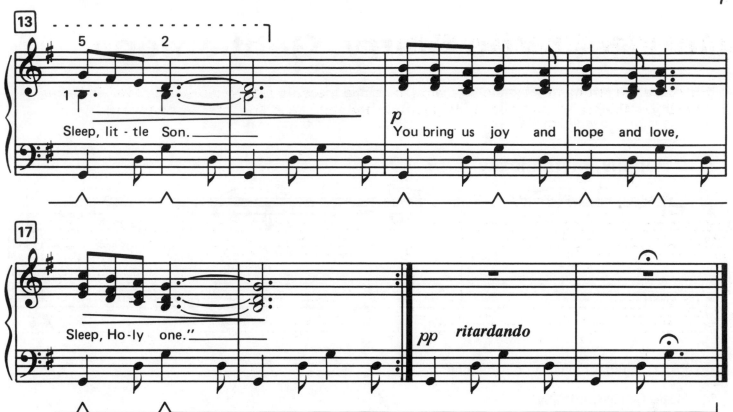

Sleep, lit - tle Son. ___ You bring us joy and hope and love,

Sleep, Ho - ly one." ___ *pp* *ritardando*

DUET PART:

Andante moderato

Play this part 8va throughout

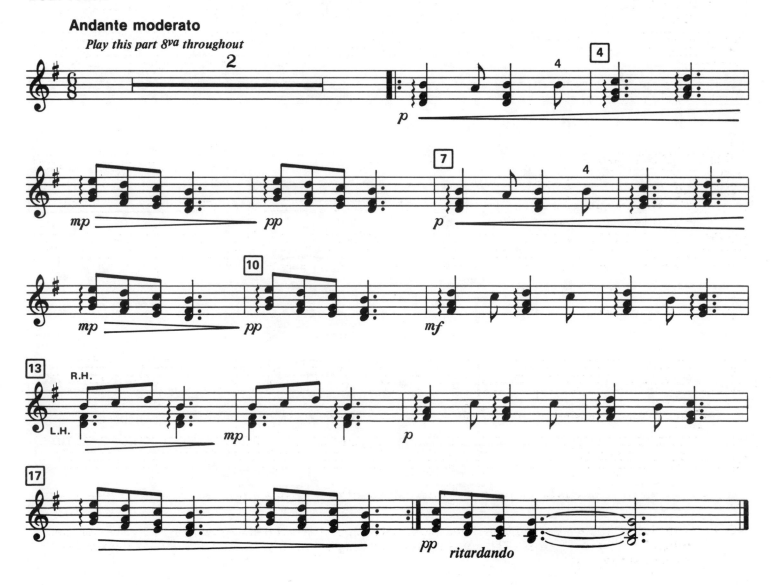

God Rest You Merry, Gentlemen

KEY OF E MINOR
Key Signature: one sharp (F♯)

Traditional

Happily, rhythmically

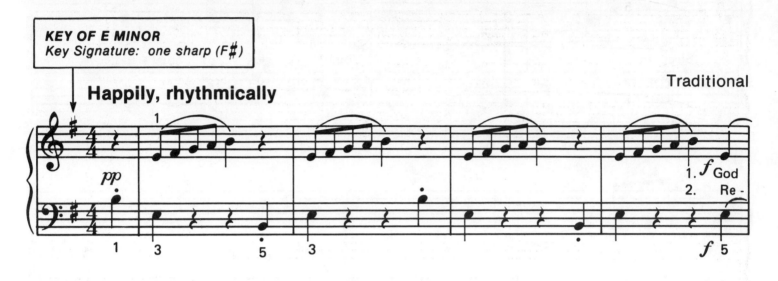

DUET PART: (Student plays 1 octave higher.)

Happily, rhythmically

March of the Three Kings

KEY OF D MINOR
Key Signature: 1 flat (B♭)

March tempo

Traditional

f (not legato)

DUET PART: (Student plays 1 octave higher.)

March tempo

(not legato)   f   L.H.

1.   (To next strain)

2.   ritardando - - - - - - - Fine

D.C. al Fine

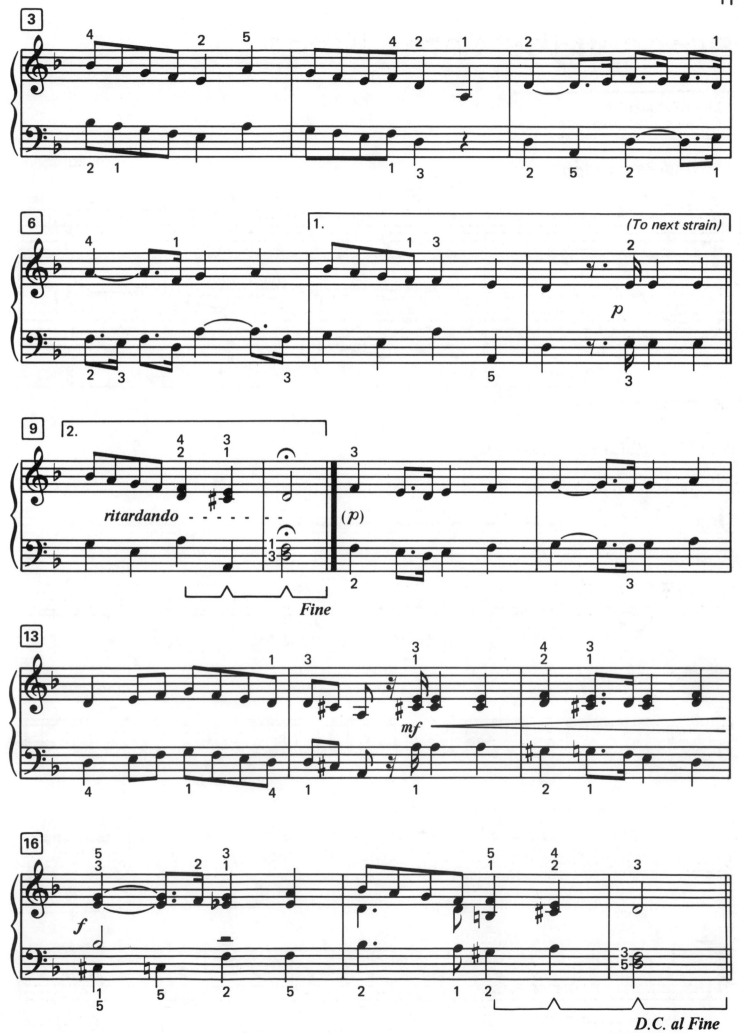

Silent Night

KEY OF B♭ MAJOR
Key signature: 2 flats (B♭ & E♭)

Franz Gruber

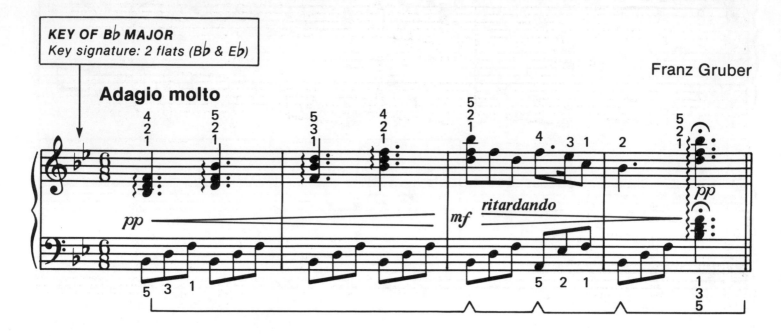

DUET PART: (Student plays 1 octave higher.)

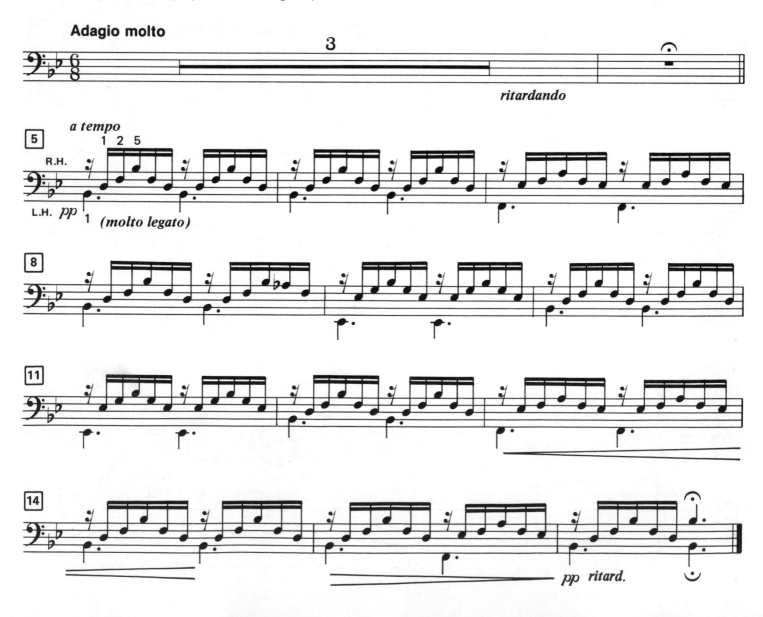

Foom, Foom, Foom!*

KEY OF G MINOR
Key signature: 2 flats (B♭ & E♭)

Traditional

Brightly & rhythmically

On De-cem-ber five and twen-ty, Foom, foom, foom!

DUET PART: (Student plays 1 octave higher.)

Brightly & rhythmically

Foom! is a sound of celebration, possibly derived from the sound of a drum.

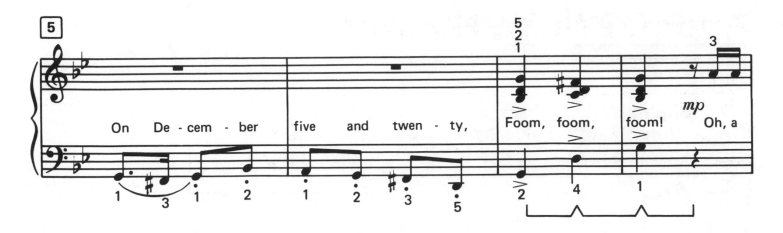

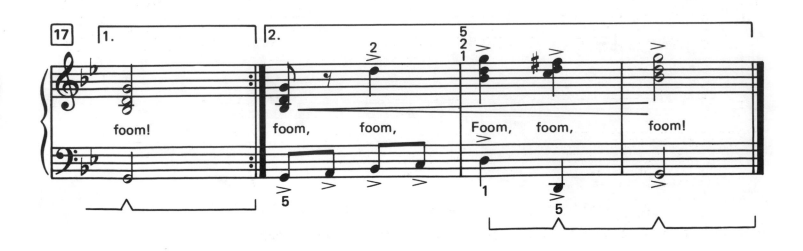

Sing Noel, Noel!

KEY OF E MINOR
Key Signature: one sharp (F♯)

Traditional

DUET PART: (Student plays 1 octave higher.)